WHO IS JESUS?

WHO IS JESUS?

A Historical and Biblical Perspective of Jesus Christ for Both the New and Seasoned Christian

MICHAEL OAKLEY AND RACHEL OAKLEY

Mission Blvd Publishing

Table of Contents

Introduction

The name "Jesus" has been used in many different ways and by multitudes of people over millennia. Who is Jesus, really? Why do so many believe in a man who lived thousands of years ago in a place and time completely different from our world today? Could you personally ever consider saying that you know Jesus?

Let us imagine you have only heard that Jesus lived somewhat two thousand years ago. You might be wondering why this book is titled "Who *Is* Jesus?" instead of "Who *Was* Jesus?" You might have heard a lot of people talk about Jesus enthusiastically, skeptically, or outright confusingly. You may even have been drawn to this book because you like talking about Jesus and want to have better words to communicate what you are trying to say.

Rest assured, this book will have what you need to get started on who Jesus is. As a married couple, we Oakleys have a deep passion for Jesus and a heartfelt fire for helping people in their relationship with Jesus. This is the essence of the gospel; it is the good news of God loving us and wanting to be close and personal with each and every person. We will unpack the evidence, Scripture, logic, and life-applicable meaning of who Jesus is. We believe Jesus wants every person to make an informed decision to believe in Him and follow Him, knowing who He is and what it would mean to become His disciple before committing to that evermore. He called it taking up our own cross daily to follow Him, which means there is a manner of sacrifice of self, and subjecting ourselves to His heart and plan, in faith that it is the greater good. Have you made such a decision? Do you think you ever will? Are you wondering if Jesus was ever even a real person? And where do we begin looking to know who He is when it is not like we can send Him a friend request on an app?

The persona, personality, and being of Jesus have multiple facets, much like we experience in ourselves. Waking up in the morning, we could be a barista and cook first, then a husband or wife, then a worker and colleague, and on weekends, we get to actively be friends—our "role" changes throughout the day or week based on the situation. Are we a different person every time we speak to someone new? No, our being doesn't change, just the applicable expression of who we are in relation to the person/s we are expressing ourselves to. Our journey between these pages of who Jesus is will look at the same phenomena. Jesus is the same from eternity unto eternity, but how we have, and each continue to, experience Him has multiple sides to the same diamond, all glorious and precious above all else.

We will walk you through who Jesus is from a historical perspective, putting into context the time and place of His birth, death, ministry, and people. We will discuss definitions of Jesus such as "the Son of God," our Friend, Lover, Healer, humble Servant, His Human nature, and (most of all) what it means to say that He is our Savior. This will involve discussing what brilliant minds and incredible people have discovered about historical evidence for Jesus and who Jesus claimed to be according to the accounts available. There will also be discussions on who He has been *proven* to be—these will remain up to you, as the reader, to evaluate and interpret in your own life. Lastly, there will be some diving into what some people have said about Jesus over many years, which we simply do not believe to be true.

Throughout this journey, we will introduce you to various topics, areas of study, concepts, or worldviews that may not be tackled in their full depth on these pages. However, we encourage every one of our readers to take in all that is said here with a sound mind and calmly evaluate it on your own time, especially if that inspires you to go digging deeper through other sources or the works of wonderful people who focused specifically on what you find yourself wanting to know more about.

Are you new to the faith and seeking a life-applicable exposition of who Jesus is? Do you feel like you haven't got the tools yet to put the whole Biblical picture together yourself? Or are you seasoned in the faith after many years of living as a believer and always looking for more detail and clarity on how to express to the world around you the root of your joy in eternal life?

As a matter of principle and faith, the primary source and reference for this endeavor will be the Bible. The Bible is a compilation of books (sixty-six as the primary canon) that were written by people spanning dozens of authors, centuries, various geographical locations, and historical contexts, and recorded and copied faithfully and trustworthily by the most devoted of groups. After millennia, the margin of error between any manuscripts as close to the original as we could find and today rests solely in minor syntaxes and none that affect the meaning of the text. The Bible is divided into two primary categories: the Old and New Testaments, which basically refer to before and after Jesus. These are collections of what people wrote about the lives and historical events of certain people (focused on the descendants of Abraham, Isaac, and Jacob—the ancestors of Israel) and how they thought, felt, experienced, and expressed God throughout their lives. It is not a collection of limiting regulations, sermons, and boring historical records—it is a living lens into the lives of people who walked with God, Jesus, and the Holy Spirit. The Bible contains their joys, fears, mistakes, reconciliation, prayers, problems, successes, and so much more! And it brings us to a knowledge of who God is by what is written of Him as He made Himself known to people personally all throughout human history.

Gaining a clear perspective of who Jesus claimed to be, proved to be, was thought to be, and is misrepresented as, is what you can expect from these pages. Getting the opportunity to discover the realities of who Jesus is in relation to your own life and what that means is what we want to invite you to unwrap with us.

Whether you currently agree with this statement is a matter open within your heart, but we believe Jesus is real, personal, and can be closely known as Friend, God, and anything in between. So, it is our hope that you will enjoy this journey and make the most of what may come to you in the pages ahead.

CHAPTER 1

Jesus in Historical Context

Diving into any discussion on who Jesus is requires an important starting premise that is often overlooked—Jesus is real. It would be meaningless to build a whole book about someone who isn't real, especially from the perspective of an eternal value attached to this subject matter. That will be the focus of this chapter. We will be aiming to define if and that Jesus is real. That includes illustrating that Jesus truly walked this earth, truly died, and truly rose from the dead. Why those three things?

The Biblical claim that sets Christianity apart from any other worldview, religion, or spiritual structure is that Jesus is God in full, who became fully human for our sake, lived a complete human life, died an unwarranted death as a sacrifice for all sin, and was raised from the dead to heal the divide that our sin brought between God and us (Hebrews chapter 9 and 10, in the New Testament). Thereby, to prove that Jesus is real, we have to "prove" all of these points. Only proving a subset of these key identifiers to Jesus will mean that we haven't proven Jesus— in the full Biblical sense and intent of who Christians claim to believe in—to actually be real. Proving Jesus was a real human with good moral teachings would fall greatly short of the Biblical and Christian stance of who Jesus claimed to be: the Son of God and the only way to the Father, to eternal life, the One who brings the Spirit of God into our lives fully. Even considering Jesus to be an exceptional Prophet of God is not enough. There are two options, really. If Jesus was not who He said He was, then we shouldn't trust anything He said since He would clearly have been deceived and delusional. If Jesus said anything of value, the sensibility of those words would probably be found in a more trust-worthy source than a deceived or delusional man. Or, if Jesus is who He said He is, then we need to absolutely trust every last bit of what He said since it is assuredly of eternal and immeasurable value. There is no middle ground.

Now, how does one go about this task? Firstly, we will look for evidence that there was a man named Jesus who lived approximately two thousand years ago in the regions of Israel. Secondly, we will look at the accounts available of His words and actions and assess their reliability. Thirdly, we will assess the evidence of His death. Lastly, we will discuss the matter of His resurrection. If all of these conclude an objective truth, then that allows for the personal decision on whether we can or will believe in Him.

Who Jesus Is Accepted to Be

Have you ever heard of people in historical accounts from centuries or millennia ago and wondered how true or accurate these accounts are? Have you ever listened to court cases and how closely the judge and the jury will assess and compare eyewitness accounts with alibis and allegations? Have you ever wondered if the story a person is telling you is being told the way it actually happened?

There have always been questions regarding whether Jesus was real or not. Truly, the people who lived and learned with Him in the first century would be the best (and only) people who can confirm this. The rest of us face the struggle of not only having to decide whether to believe or not, but first, we have to accept whether there is a real person to believe in—and Jesus knew this. That is why Jesus told His disciples that they are blessed, but those who believe even without having seen

Him, that is a true faith indeed (the Gospel of John 20:24–30 in the New Testament).

From the viewpoints of various beliefs, other religions, and secular circles, there are a few undeniable facts about Jesus. These are agreed upon by historical scholarly experts from a wide range of demographics and sources. The sources that provide historical evidence for the existence, actions, and teachings of people like Julius Caesar or Plato (by definition of modern text analysis methods that even the crime investigators use to determine the validity of an account) are less credible (fewer remaining accounts, and with a longer timespan between the events and the earliest available account) than the sources for Jesus' life. Josephus, a Jewish historian who would have had no personal motive to corroborate the story of Jesus, wrote accurate and verifiable details of the social implications that this man had at that time. The "differences" in the gospel accounts ascertain that they were not concocted by a mob with a motive but reflect the narrative of authentic participants in the story being told from various perspectives. By all of these accounts, and many others as well (Windle, 2022), Jesus is accepted to be a Jewish man who was born in Bethlehem, and lived into adulthood in a town called Nazareth in Israel, some roughly two thousand years ago. It is accepted that Jesus started moving around the towns of Israel when He was in His thirties (approximately) and began a movement that sparked lots of controversies. Israel was under Roman rule at that time, and both Jewish and Roman historians have accounts of Jesus and the news that spread of Him. It is accepted that this controversy reached a peak around the Pascha festival of the Jewish community in Jerusalem circa 33 A.D, which led to the crucifixion of Jesus. Furthermore, the accounts of Jesus's beatings, mockery, time on the cross, and eventual death on the cross are clear and undeniable. In methods and findings that weren't known to the people of that time yet, the medical evidence indicates that Jesus died on the cross by asphyxiation before the spear was stuck into His side (Strobel, 1998). This is generally where the historians' consensus stops because accepting the resurrection as historically true would require an acceptance of Jesus for who He claimed to be. However, we can discuss what the further accounts of Jesus are and why so many do believe these are credible and true.

Who Jesus Claimed to Be and Why He Was Persecuted

The Gospel accounts (the first four books of the New Testament, written summaries of Jesus's life and teachings) make a few things particularly clear about Jesus. One of the things that always blows my mind is how each of the four Gospel authors had their personal emphasis on what they focused on more regarding Jesus (Pawson, 2017). Matthew was a Jewish man who had collected taxes (people strongly disliked tax collectors, even in those days), who wrote to a Jewish audience and ended up focusing a lot on how Jesus fulfilled the Law and Prophets by being the promised Messiah. Mark wrote to a Gentile (all non-Jews) audience and placed emphasis on Jesus being the One to restore *all people* to a right-standing relationship with God. Luke was a physician who wrote his account of Jesus as a letter of defense when Paul was in prison, so he wrote more about what Jesus did to affirm His claims of who He is. John was the disciple of Jesus who would live the longest and be the oldest. John wrote his Gospel (derived from the Greek word *euangelion* for "good news") at the very end of the first-century A.D. By then, various false teachings and skew practices had already crept into the church, so John focused on how Jesus is eternal, has always been the same, and that true faith in Him is a faith of selfless love at all times.

The Messiah had been prophesied since the start of human history. Part of God's declaration to Eve, after their fall into sin, is that there would come a seed (the singular is used) from her whose heel will be bitten by the snake (the Accuser/Tempter, "Satan" in Hebrew), but this Seed will also trample on the snake's head. For Abraham, the patriarch of the nation of Israel (and others), God made the promise, at almost a hundred years old, that he would have a son, descendants as many as the stars in the night sky, and through his seed (again, singular, referring to a specific person very clearly) all the nations of the world will be blessed. A while down the line, the prophecies regarding the Messiah expanded as God spoke through His prophets. One particular prophecy would be that this Messiah would come from the bloodline of King David and would establish a kingdom even greater, better, and stronger than the one Israel had under David's rule. There are many prophecies about the Messiah scattered throughout the whole Old Testament, and various people have done detailed studies into this (Jesus Film Project, 2021 & Pawson, 2017). However, what is very clear is that Jesus' claim to be the Messiah (John chapters 8 and 18 present this clearly) was controversial and surprising to the Jews. Why is that? What did they expect?

The responses from the Jewish leaders, right up to the mockery Jesus suffered as He hung on the cross, showed some key factors. The Jewish people had endured a long history of social, military, and judicial oppression from various rulers—the time of the Judges, King Saul, the unstable times after King Solomon, and then after the destruction of Jerusalem, and even after their return from exile into Babylon. At the time of Jesus, they were held under the Roman thumb. Primarily, many Israelites and Jewish believers in general (even the Greek, "Hellenistic" Jews) were expecting the Messiah to come blazing into Jerusalem with an army behind and overthrow the oppressive political rulers to establish an Israelite kingdom again. They were expecting a warlord like David and more! They had very deep awareness and knowledge of the Messianic prophecies (Matthew chapter 2 and Psalm 22 referenced in Matthew 27, for example), but their expectations did not match what Jesus was doing and preaching.

Keeping these in mind, when we read about Jesus in the New Testament, he claims to be a number of key theological and spiritual roles. All of them are important, and we encourage you to look into the New Testament at those beyond what we have room for here.

Certainly, the most controversial, even offensive, claim Jesus made was to call Himself the "Son of God" (Matthew chapter 26). This did not happen only later in life; Jesus spoke about God as His Father in a more direct and personal sense than anyone else from a young age (Luke chapter 2). To the Israelites, this claim of being "One with God" while walking on the earth, as a man of skin and bones who they knew from birth, was blasphemy of the highest degree. They believe, at their core, "God is One" (Deuteronomy chapter 6), and this claim shattered that principle from their understanding, but God Himself affirmed it (Matthew chapters 3 and Mark chapter 9). Next, Jesus came with a message of repentance, "*From then on Jesus began to preach, 'Repent, because the kingdom of heaven has come near'*" (*Christian Standard Bible*, 2017, Matthew 4:17), and with a view on life that challenges people to an incredible degree to reassess their views of what is good, true, and Godly (Bruce, 1983). Most prophets do that, technically, so what else made Jesus so different? The second claim Jesus made that caused great confusion and offense among the Pharisees, Sadducees, and many Jewish people in general, was that He claimed to be the One who can judge and forgive sin on the Father's authority (look at the encounter in Mark chapter 2). However, Jesus did make it clear that His primary mission was not that of judging and condemning sinners but actually of redeeming sinners (all of humanity) into a position of available and intimate relationship with God (John chapters 3, 12, and 17). That was the third offense—to the Jew, the idea of not doing your own penance for your own sin through your own offering was strange and bewildering.

Ironically, all three of these are still the same reasons why many don't accept Jesus in the twenty-first century. The concept of a "Three-In-One" God (Triune, "*three in person, one in essence,*" a wording that was only settled upon theologically centuries after Jesus' ministry) seems confusing, to say the least. The simplicity seems to be that God, throughout history, Scripture, and our personal experience (yours also?), makes Himself known to us in exactly that fashion (Long, 2019). Secondly, there is no other method of redemption from sin that could "make sense" more than what Jesus claimed to be doing the whole time He was on earth, on the cross, and in His resurrected preaching (Daane, 1965). Any idea of us "earning" our way back to God through goodness is immediately undone by the mere fact that any good deed, once you believe that, is tainted by selfish desire, and thus every good deed also keeps adding to your bad deeds; not to mention the fact that our sin is immeasurably more severe through the eyes of a perfectly holy and righteous God than we could ever truly perceive them to be. Thirdly, a proper understanding of what Jesus' aim was is key. Many think that "salvation" is a rescue mission or your soul out of the fires of hell, while it is really the love story of a Gentleman pursuing one who is precious to Him. We will explore this in a later section.

Who Jesus Is Shown to Be

We mentioned the prophecies fulfilled, and these are exceptionally interesting to dive into. In this segment, we will look at the things Jesus did that showed who He is. Read this like you would a biography; you want to get to know the character, the heart, the mannerisms, and the personality of a person that someone else is telling you about through their words. "Actions speak louder than words," the saying goes—so what do Jesus' actions show about who He is?

The four Gospel accounts have different first signs: a wedding where water was turned into wine, a man delivered from a demon right in a synagogue, various healings and deliverances, or claiming Isaiah 61 onto Himself. All these, however, had one thing in common: they were uncommon, unheard of, impossible to replicate or conceive in the people's minds, and yet they very clearly happened. Whenever God did anything in the Old Testament, it was mostly motivated by getting people to see and "know that I AM the Lord God of Israel," the one and only God. Jesus does much the same. Every healing, every teaching, every deliverance, and every miracle (walking on water, multiplying bread and fish until basketfuls of leftovers are picked up) all share the common purpose of growing people's faith in Him. The mere fact that Jesus never focused people onto Himself, but pointed them toward God through Him, should show Him to be the Messiah, the One to reconcile humanity with God. He astounded people with wisdom (Caesar's coin), care (Lazarus, or the little girl, raised from the dead in love, compassion, and faith), mercy (the woman caught in adultery, the woman at the well), while also heralding in a deeper perspective on righteousness (Matthew chapters 5 through 7) than they ever thought or lived! We are used to these "stories," but they all really are miracles that should, by any human means, be entirely impossible. The number of prophecies fulfilled and historical, archeological, or later scientific evidence only add to the affirmations of who He is. He doesn't show Himself to be the Savior of the whole world by just dying on a cross, but by *living a whole life* on our level. God (very clearly, by what He could do!) Himself walked as and among men, growing tired, hungry, and tempted but overcoming it! He is shown to be the Savior not just by His sacrifice on the cross but by all the countless daily sacrifices He undertook for our sake so that, when He washed our sins away, He could also clothe us with the perfection of His righteousness that He lived and modeled for a whole lifetime on our behalf!

John the Baptist sent his disciples to ask Jesus whether He really is the One Israel has been waiting for.

Jesus replied to them, 'Go and report to John what you hear and see: The blind receive their sight, the lame walk, those with leprosy are cleansed, the deaf hear, the dead are raised, and the poor are told the good news, and blessed is the one who isn't offended by me.' (Christian Standard Bible, 2017, Matthew 11:4-6)

Jesus quoted the Old Testament prophet Isaiah, events that undeniably were attributed to the hailing of the era of the Messiah centuries earlier and that people could not deny (Matthew 15, CSB).

There are even those who believe that archaeological mysteries (like the *Shroud of Turin,* for example) also affirm the true death, burial, and resurrected glory of Jesus. However controversial it might have been for the people of His time, and since, to be confronted with this man claiming to be the Messiah, they could not deny the prophecies (as mentioned above) when proven. It is a difficult thing to shift your theology when all the evidence points to one answer, but your heart deeply desires another.

What Does History Tell You, Personally, About Jesus?

History proves, undoubtedly (and we encourage you to take up an endeavor on your own to look at what historical evidence there is for

Jesus from birth to death and more!), that there was a man called Jesus who gathered a large following and was crucified by Roman soldiers and the Jewish mob. History also indicates that this man's followers left ripple effects that permeated every level and corner of the world throughout the centuries with structures, beliefs, and life values that have stuck with people for generations. There seems to be ample reason to believe the accounts of Jesus being raised from the dead. The personal stories of how people's lives have been impacted seem to be another viable piece of evidence for His being real, alive, and Who He said He is. This, however, is a more personal consideration, an open-ended subject for you, the reader, to ponder as we discuss the following chapters.

CHAPTER 2

Jesus, the Son of God

We would love to have dealt more with the historical evidence for this remarkable Man. However, Jesus is so much more than an ancient pharaoh or warlord to study just with historical evidence—He is alive and personal. That is the core message of the Bible: God is alive, personal, and intentional about wanting *you* to know Him. The Holy Spirit of God is alive and personally involved in our lives every day and so much more when we yield to His guidance. So, if this was so clear and evident throughout all of Scripture, why was Jesus crucified for preaching it? Jesus claimed what no one else would ever dream of: to be the eternal and only Son of God, born by a woman, raised on earth like the rest of the children, slept and ate and felt emotions, and still being entirely One with His Father in heaven by the Spirit.

Have you ever read through the whole Old Testament? Have you found some parts of it immensely confusing? We all have, and that is partly the point. The Old Testament was written by people led by God's Spirit (see Paul's second letter to Timothy, especially chapter 2). He alone knew the exact plan ahead, but He hid Jesus in the story with Israel the whole time. Every person, in some way or another, would play an undeniably important role in His redemption plan. For example, the Hebrew people believed that they were inspired to give their children names at birth, which were believed to hold meaning—spoiler, they do! When we map just the meaning of a few names (BibleCodes, n.d.), we find glimpses of God's salvation narrative. The first ten names of the Bible mean: "*The God-Man is appointed, a mortal man of sorrow is born! The Glory of God shall come down, instructing that His death shall bring those in despair, comfort, and rest!*" This can be mapped even further, all the way to Jesus, outlining the story exactly through some people who themselves, let alone their parents, could never have planned how most of their lives/lineage could play out.

Even better, not all times when God prepared the way for His people to receive their Messiah were as obscured. We have briefly mentioned the Old Testament prophecies about Jesus, and these pointed to Him, but did you know there are moments *showing* the eternal Jesus already in the Old Testament, alive and active with God the Father and the Spirit? Genesis says, "*Then God said, 'Let us make man in our image, according to our likeness'*" (*Christian Standard Bible*, 2017, Genesis 1:26). This is not a definite indication of the Godhead as the Trinity according to Christian beliefs, but it is the start. There are the appearances of the "Son of Man," a title dedicated by God and reserved for a heavenly being who, by the title, is also a Man (Kümmel, 1976), and clear as crystal is associated with the Messiah (Daniel chapter 7, and Matthew 12 verses 15–21).

There are also many other instances where, looking back, we can clearly see how precisely God had outlined the person and ministry of the Messiah through, primarily, family relations. We see this in the noble act of Judah (Genesis chapter 44) standing up to take the place of his younger brother, and since then, the prophecy was made—and proven true in Jesus—that the Messiah would be born from the line of Judah. We see the sonship declared by the ministry of the priests, especially the High Priest's succession, as God ordained it since Exodus. We can notice the redemptive value being followed in the story of Rahab, who would form part of the line that carried David and eventually Jesus. God showed His mercy and grace abundantly in the case of David and Solomon. David had given into temptation and had an affair with a married woman (Bathsheba), who fell pregnant with his child, but David had the man die in battle to try and cover up his sin. God's severe justice was rightfully practiced through this child's death, but His mercy and grace shone through when He appointed Solomon, born from Bathsheba, to succeed David. They were Israel's two most notable kingships ever. I have taken these two tangents at the outset of this chapter for a specific purpose. In order to believe that Jesus is the Son of God, we need to hear God, and Jesus, substantiate this claim. If Jesus claimed it, but God never affirmed it, we would have good reason to doubt it. And if Jesus never claimed or affirmed it, then we have no reason to think it. But if they both claim and affirm it, then we have no excuse not to believe it.

Now, what would it mean for Jesus to be the "Son of God," the "only One like Him ever to be born" (Gospel of John, chapters 1 through 3)? The Old Testament paved the way for the coming of the Messiah, the Savior, the Son of God, ultimately culminating in the prophetic ministry of John the Baptist, who saw and announced the arrival of Jesus (Luke chapter 3).

Spending some brief time to look up and reflect on a few New Testament passages, what can you gather from these regarding Jesus' eternal sonship to God and relationship to the Spirit?

God, speaking to the prophet Nathan to repeat this to David, said:

Furthermore, I declare to you that the Lord himself will build a house for you. When your time comes to be with your ancestors, I will raise up after you your descendant, who is one of your own sons, and I will establish his kingdom. He is the one who will build a house for me, and I will establish his throne forever. I will be his father, and he will be my son. I will not remove my faithful love from him as I removed it from the one who was before you. I will appoint him over my house and my kingdom forever, and his throne will be established forever. (*Christian Standard Bible*, 2017, 1 Chronicles 17.10–14)

Solomon, widely accepted (Pawson, 2017), wrote in his poetic musings, known to us as *Proverbs* (and we recommend you read Proverbs regularly, a few verses or a chapter a day even; these words digest slowly, but we believe they hold immense value), the following about God:

Who has gone up to heaven and come down?

Who has gathered the wind in his hands?
Who has bound up the waters in a cloak?
Who has established all the ends of the earth?
What is his name,
and what is the name of his son—
if you know? (*Christian Standard Bible*, 2017, Proverbs 30:4)

There are two instances in the Gospels where God, from a heavenly voice, declared Jesus to be His Son. One at His baptism, the other on a mount with His disciples Peter, James, and John. At the Baptism of Jesus, God said:

When Jesus was baptized, he went up immediately from the water. The heavens suddenly opened for him, and he saw the Spirit of God descending like a dove and coming down on him. And a voice from heaven said, "This is my beloved Son, with whom I am well-pleased." (*Christian Standard Bible*, 2017, Matthew 3:16–17)

On the mount, God said, "*A cloud appeared, overshadowing them, and a voice came from the cloud: 'This is my beloved Son; listen to him!'*" (*Christian Standard Bible*, 2017, Mark 9:7), and, "*While he was saying this, a cloud appeared and overshadowed them. They became afraid as they entered the cloud. Then a voice came from the cloud, saying, 'This is my Son, the Chosen One; listen to him!'*" (*Christian Standard Bible*, 2017, Luke 9:34-35), and Matthew also later recorded, "*While he was still speaking, suddenly a bright cloud covered them, and a voice from the cloud said, 'This is my beloved Son, with whom I am well-pleased. Listen to him!' When the disciples heard this, they fell facedown and were terrified*" (*Christian Standard Bible*, 2017, Matthew 17:5-6). We encourage you to go read these full accounts in their respective chapters to take in the full context. All three of these writers had separate histories, focal points, and audiences, yet, they all have exactly the same account (Kümmel, 1976). What do these declarations of God say or mean to you?

There are two other points we also want to illustrate before we draw any conclusions on this: one, the origin or birth of Jesus, and two, others who had also declared and identified Him as the Son of God.

Follow this up by reading the full Luke chapter 3. The angel Gabriel (often seen throughout the Old Testament) appeared to Zechariah, a priest, and declared he would have a son in his old age, and this son would be like the prophet Elijah to make the people ready to receive their Messiah. The angel also appeared to a young, engaged, virgin lady.

Then the angel told her, "Do not be afraid, Mary, for you have found favor with God. Now listen: You will conceive and give birth to a son, and you will name him Jesus. He will be great and will be called the Son of the Most High, and the Lord God will give him the throne of his father David. He will reign over the house of Jacob forever, and his kingdom will have no end." (Christian Standard Bible, 2017, Luke 1:30–33)

He explained this to her, and when she became pregnant, her husband-to-be wanted to depart from the matter but not destroy her honor by secretly divorcing her (or breaking off the engagement, basically). Joseph, however, was told in a dream what Mary had been told and that he should take care of her and the Child, the same method God used to guide Joseph to move to Egypt for a while when Jesus would not have been safe as a small boy in Israel. However, this is not Jesus' true origin, as He is eternal (Gospel of John chapter 1 and Revelation chapter 1).

How many others declared Jesus to be the Son of God? There were the wise men who read the signs of God's prophecies and found Jesus soon after His birth, and the same with the shepherds to whom angels appeared with the good news. There were Zechariah and Elizabeth, John's (the Baptist) parents. The two devout people, Simeon and Anna, who both served prophetically by the Holy Spirit upon them (Luke chapter 2) and who identified Jesus as the Savior, Messiah, the Son of God in beautiful and compassionate, sincere and true, praise and worship of God. John the Baptist, as was his whole mission, identified and presented Jesus to the people.

The next day John saw Jesus coming toward him and said, "Look, the Lamb of God, who takes away the sin of the world! This is the one I told you about: 'After me comes a man who ranks ahead of me, because he existed before me.' I didn't know him, but I came baptizing with water so that he might be revealed to Israel." And John testified, "I saw the Spirit descending from heaven like a dove, and he rested on him. I didn't know him, but he who sent me to baptize with water told me, 'The one you see the Spirit descending and resting on—he is the one who baptizes with the Holy Spirit.' I have seen and testified that this is the Son of God." (Christian Standard Bible, 2017, John 1:29–34)

Jesus also had close friends, like Lazarus, with his sisters Mary and Martha, to whom He had said (after the death and just before the resurrection of Lazarus, which was one of Jesus' miracles).

Jesus said to her, "I am the resurrection and the life. The one who believes in me, even if he dies, will live. Everyone who lives and believes in me will never die. Do you believe this?" "Yes, Lord," she told him, "I believe you are the Messiah, the Son of God, who comes into the world." (Christian Standard Bible, 2017, John 11:25–27)

There were also many others throughout the Gospel account who, either by the demons within them or by the Spirit's revelation of truth to them, proclaimed Jesus to be the Son of God after being healed or delivered from various ailments.

There are many examples to look at beyond these few—but what do these already tell you? How do you think you, if you were a Jew in that time who read and knew and memorized the Scriptures, would respond to this man and His claims to be the Son of God? I believe God, Jesus, and the Holy Spirit are all known throughout the whole Bible. I believe there is sufficient reason to believe Jesus is who He says He is. However, even in light of all these declarations, people usually look for a sign themselves (Matthew chapters 12 and 16), but the one guaranteed sign that most, if not all, who have ever claimed to believe in Jesus affirm is that of personal testimony—when Jesus, beyond a shadow of a doubt, shows up in your own life and shakes the foundations with more love and life than you can comprehend. Would you consider Jesus to be the Son of God? Would you consider calling on Him as the Son of God in the role and authority He holds? Would you believe me if I told you that you can, that He wants you to, and that He will be your closest friend when you do?

CHAPTER 3

Jesus, Our Friend

What makes a good friend? They say, "You are the average of your five closest friends." Would that mean that a good friend is one who makes us better? Is it someone who cares so deeply for you that you know, wherever they go, they've got your back and will come at a moment's notice? Is it someone that you only spend time with for a few minutes a month and say, "Well, that's enough of you now. I need to go live my life," or someone you want to talk to as long and often as possible? What do you think it meant for Jesus' disciples when, after just over three years of living and walking and ministering with Jesus every day, He told them, "I now call you friends," or when it says that Abraham was considered a friend of God, or when it was noted that God spoke to Moses as with a friend (John 15, James 2, and Exodus 33)? Would you ever think of God Almighty as a close, intimate friend? Let us dive into the Biblical definition of friendship with Christ and then make an informed decision.

Biblical Friendship

For a Biblical understanding of *friendship*, we can turn to Solomon's (mainly, though some other people did provide insights into this book) wisdom in the book of Proverbs. Friendship is classified, motivated, or identified as true and good. Friendship:

- emphasizes building love and trust, often by covering wrongs (Proverbs 17:9)
- does not fluctuate or run away at the sight of trouble (Proverbs 17:17)
- is not found *en masse,* but there will be a few true friends (Proverbs 18:24)
- has their intentions, values, and priorities straight (Proverbs 22:11)
- does not hold back harsh truth, but with good fruit as the result of love (Proverbs 27:6)
- will be close and dependable (Proverbs 27:10) and must be kept so

This is by no means a completely exhaustive list of what the Bible recommends for friendships. However, we can begin to gather some foundational principles to look for what we define as friendship moving forward. Firstly, there is no mention anywhere of the amount of time spent together; friends can be close and true without having known each other very long. Secondly, there is the core principle of alignment —are you and your friends on the same page on the important stuff? Whenever our deepest truths, values, and priorities differ, relationships will fade and drift over time. In order to secure true, faithful, lasting friendships, an agreement on the same key points of life seems critical. Thirdly, friends don't rely on superficial things to derive value from the friendship—true friends "get their hands dirty" together, they fight things out, they wrestle with life's troubles together, they address each other earnestly, and they seek the best for each other no matter what, even if that means having a heart-piercing conversation now and then.

Jesus With the People of His Time

These are some key attributes and moments of how Jesus dealt with the people of His time as a friend.

- Jesus got people excited about spending time with Him but never misled them about what that would entail (John 1:43–51 and Matthew 4:18–22).
- Jesus placed emphasis on relationships. He did not assign a value to a relationship purely based on familial or social relation but on commitment, trust, and sincere love (Matthew 12:46–50).
- Jesus truly comforted those He ministered to and walked with. He didn't just give a quick response to settle the situation; He took care of their hearts, souls, and spirits with as much time and attention as required. Comfort also refers to the Latin root of the word used when it was first translated from Greek into English Bibles—*with power*, to strengthen, to give hope and capacity for renewed zeal in action (John 8:1–11, and John 4–6).
- Jesus focused on the individual. He never glanced over the person who was with Him at that moment in preparation for the next or over-generalized His ministry to suit the masses but missed the heart of the individual's needs (John 9, Mark 1:39–45, Mark 2:1–12, and Luke 8).
- The friendship that Jesus modeled with His disciples showed that friendship comes with regular communication. We pick this up throughout the gospels as He spoke and discoursed with His disciples throughout the years over long journeys and hearty meals.
- Jesus never set any requirements for people to have to "rise to His level." The whole principle behind everything Jesus did is God coming to meet us where we are. God never requires us to change anything to come to Him. As we are, He reaches out to us, calling us to Him with open arms and a smile of complete sincere joy to welcome us into His presence. When Jesus called His disciples, there were no qualifications or competency tests—He just called them, and they had to do nothing but accept the invitation.

- By extension of the previous point, it is also true that Jesus, like any friend, has an influence on those who are close to Him. His character will rub off on those who spend time with Him. His heart, mind, and ways will become more and more part of how His followers/friends feel, think, and act. This is, however, better than any other friend possible since we do not have to wonder whether the characteristics and mannerisms we pick up are good or bad—this is God Almighty Himself, who created you, who knows you better than you ever could, who is being intentional and devoted with every step of the journey He takes with each of us to bring out the utmost best of what He knows He put within us.

We can see even more examples of Jesus being the BFF, in the most literal sense possible, to those around Him throughout the Gospel accounts. But the "excuse" can easily be made for, "but they knew Him in person, saw Him every day, physically walked and ate with Him; how can I have the same friendship?" For that, there is a two-part answer. One, people were able to have a similar relationship with God before they walked with Jesus in person (comparably, not exactly). Two, and more applicable to us today, the remainder of the New Testament teaches us exactly how to have this same relationship perpetually, now that this relationship is available to us after His resurrection and ascension.

Friendship With God

Throughout the Bible, God does use the comparison of friendship to make His true self, His best intentions, understandable at our level. Here is a list of Scriptures that we recommend you read up on in your own time and see what character of God you can map out through the Old Testament of God as a friend and His advice for us regarding friendships.

- Proverbs 3:32
- Genesis 2
- Genesis 6 through 9
- Genesis 17 and 18
- Exodus 3 and 4
- Exodus 19 and 20
- Exodus 32 and 33
- Joshua 1
- Joshua 10:1–15
- 1 Samuel 1 through 3
- 1 Samuel 8
- 1 Samuel 13
- 1 Samuel 16 and 17
- 1 Samuel 20
- 2 Samuel 7
- 2 Samuel 9
- 1 Kings 3
- 1 Kings 8:1 up to 1 Kings 9:9
- 1 Kings 11
- 1 Kings 17 through 19
- 2 Kings 1 and 2
- 2 Kings 17
- Job 38 through 42
- Habakkuk 1 through 3

Jesus as Friend of the Whole Church

When Jesus died, was resurrected, and ascended into heaven, He sent the Holy Spirit to enable, steer, and strengthen the church (those who believe in Him) as their lives and journeys progressed in this newly given righteousness that enabled true relationship and worship with and of God (John 4:21–26). As they went in various directions, teaching people about all of this, they founded new communities of believers (churches and congregations). Later, they would write letters to follow up with these people on how things were progressing, to comment on some key matters that they felt needed reiteration, or just provide some instructional guidance on life as believers. It is in these letters that we find the values of Jesus being our friend even today, through the Spirit and by our relationship with God Three-in-One (Romans 1).

One of the first matters to consider here is that as much of a friend He may be, He is still God. Thus, His standards and values and ways and decisions do not shift. He meets us where we are, He accommodates our frame of understanding, and He works with us gently—but we could never think of moving *His* target of right and good to *our* preferences. If one must move to match the other in this friendship, it will be us. Therefore, truly being a friend of Jesus will involve detaching ourselves from the world and many things we may have previously enjoyed (alone or with other people) in order to do together what God enjoys, recommends, and desires when it comes to spending time with His church (Romans 6–8 and Romans 12–15).

From the pen of a "half-brother" of Jesus, James, we find that another big portion of Jesus' friendship is that there is no favoritism (James 2). It is God's desire to have a relationship with *everyone* so that "none would perish." Friendship with Jesus, the Spirit, and the Father also means that we remain humble and open to His guidance, trusting that He has our best in mind as we follow His leadership, which He doesn't give to us in the form of military orders, but in the co-operative form of a wise friend (James 4 and Ezekiel 4). From a similar familial relation, we have the words of Jude, saying:

> *But you, dear friends, as you build yourselves up in your most holy faith, praying in the Holy Spirit, keep yourselves in the love of God, waiting expectantly for the mercy of our Lord Jesus Christ for eternal life. Have mercy on those who waver; save others by snatching them from the fire; have mercy on others but with fear, hating even the garment defiled by the flesh. Now to him who is able to protect you from stumbling and to make you stand in the presence of his glory, without blemish and with great joy, to the only God our Savior, through Jesus Christ our Lord, be glory, majesty, power, and authority before all*

time, now and forever. Amen. (*Christian Standard Bible*, 2017, Jude 1:20–25)

Peter was one of Jesus' closest disciples. He wrestled with a lot of points and was often a bit stubborn or oblivious. However, the journey he went on, the mistakes he made, and the ways in which Jesus rebuked Him with sincere honesty in love evidently set him on a changed path for life. These actions of Jesus have been, for him and millions of others since then, something to be grateful for, and we can pick up on this within his letters to certain churches. As a general principle, having Jesus as our friend is a two-way street. He made Himself known to us, and we freely receive that gift and enjoy that life, but that also calls for us to make Him known to other people since the desire of a true friend will be to see their friend be happy, and Jesus is made happy by being introduced to new people who don't know Him yet. These come by words, yes, but also more substantially by actions. As Peter says:

Therefore, be alert and sober-minded for prayer. Above all, maintain constant love for one another, since love covers a multitude of sins. Be hospitable to one another without complaining. Just as each one has received a gift, use it to serve others, as good stewards of the varied grace of God. If anyone speaks, let it be as one who speaks God's words; if anyone serves, let it be from the strength God provides, so that God may be glorified through Jesus Christ in everything. (*Christian Standard Bible*, 2017, 1 Peter 4:7–11)

Friendship with Christ is best understood in the theology of Paul. Saul was a Jewish Pharisee who disliked the movement and message of the "people of the Way" (as they were known before first being called "Christians"), who was on his way to persecute some believers to death, when Jesus appeared to him and asked, "Saul, why do you persecute *Me?*" This not only led Saul of Tarsus to become an avid believer and radical preacher of the gospel of Jesus but also solidified a core concept: Christ and the church (as a whole) *are one.* We are united in Him, through His suffering, and by our faith. This implies that friendship with Jesus necessitates friendship, companionship, coworking, care, and endurance with all our fellow believers. Paul's letters are filled with illustrations and guides of these, so to discuss all of them would be to critically assess half of the New Testament. However, some of the more prominent places to find this would be in Ephesians 4, 1 Corinthians 12 through 14 as one discourse, Galatians 6, Philippians 1, 1 Thessalonians 4, and the whole of his letter to Titus.

We can also draw a valuable lesson from the short letter of Paul to Philemon on friendship. The Greek word for "brotherly love" is *phileo*, which is the root of this man's name as well. Paul starts off by stating what, I believe, any true believer and friend of Jesus and His church would want to hear at some point.

> *I always thank my God when I mention you in my prayers, because I hear of your love for all the saints and the faith that you have in the Lord Jesus. I pray that your participation in the faith may become effective through knowing every good thing that is in us for the glory of Christ. For I have great joy and encouragement from your love, because the hearts of the saints have been refreshed through you, brother.* (*Christian Standard Bible*, 2017, Philemon 1:4–7)

This letter has to do with a slave (not as bad as we picture slavery based on more recent years), a man named Onesimus, who ran away from Philemon and found his way to Paul. He came to faith in Jesus under Paul's guidance and companionship. Paul wishes to keep Onesimus in his company but knows that the right thing to do for his friend Philemon is to send Onesimus back to him first and with reconciliation. The governing thought here, however, is the value of not merely getting a man willing to work but a friend, a brother in the faith. Friendship with Jesus, and friendship with one another *in* Jesus, means that we serve one another as Jesus serves His church and receive one another as we would receive Jesus, for that is exactly who we welcome when we welcome one of His own.

Lastly, the compilation of visions, messages, and letters given by Jesus to the Apostle John (known as Revelation, the last book of the Bible) provides significant insights into Jesus' desired relationship with the ongoing church. Particularly, we can note the friendship aspects between Jesus and His church in the assistance, encouragement, and perseverance in love. However, these will be discussed in more detail regarding Jesus as Lover.

In summary, Jesus can be the greatest, most reliable, most trustworthy friend if you allow yourself to believe, rely on, and trust in Him —basically, to receive His love fully and return the utmost love you can. Many people who have grown up in the church view Jesus as this distant figure. It's understandable to do this since we don't physically see Him like the disciples did 2000 years ago. Many view Jesus as the Son of God but someone we can't be close with and have a true relationship with. A healthy and good relationship is someone you speak with on a consistent basis, share your biggest fears and problems with, and ask for help when needed. This is the friendship and relationship Jesus wants with you. A closer and deeper connection where you can come to Him in good times or bad. Jesus did not judge your past or present. He invited you to come as you are and was questioned by the Pharisees why He would eat with sinners.

As Jesus went on from there, he saw a man named Matthew sitting at the tax office, and he said to him, "Follow me," and he got up and followed him. While he was reclining at the table in the house, many tax collectors and sinners came to eat with Jesus and his disciples. When the Pharisees saw this, they asked his disciples, "Why does your teacher eat with tax collectors and sinners?" Now when he heard this, he said, "It is not those who are well who need a doctor, but those who are sick. Go and learn what this means: I desire mercy and not sacrifice. For I didn't come to call the righteous, but sinners." (Christian Standard Bible, 2017, Matthew 9:9–13)

Jesus was a friend who knew your good and your bad sides and still loved you regardless (see Luke 7, around verse 34)—the sign of a true friendship. Furthermore, however, friendship is a two-way street. We cannot think we can have Jesus as our best friend if we don't return the friendship. He asked for our faith in Him and worked with you to offer forgiveness.

As the Apostle John put it:

Dear friends, let us love one another, because love is from God, and everyone who loves has been born of God and knows God. The one who does not love does not know God, because God is love. God's love was revealed among us in this way: God sent his one and only Son into the world so that we might live through him. Love consists in this: not that we loved God, but that he loved us and sent his Son to be the atoning sacrifice for our sins. Dear friends, if God loved us in this way, we also must love one another. No one has ever seen God. If we love one another, God remains in us and his love is made complete in us. This is how we know that we remain in him and he in us: He has given us of his Spirit. And we have seen and we testify that the Father has sent his Son as the world's Savior. Whoever confesses that Jesus is the Son of God—God remains in him and he in God. And we have come to know and to believe the love that God has for us.

God is love, and the one who remains in love remains in God, and God remains in him. In this, love is made complete with us so that we may have confidence in the day of judgment, because as he is, so also are we in this world. There is no fear in love; instead, perfect love drives out fear, because fear involves punishment. So the one who fears is not complete in love. We love because he first loved us. If anyone says, 'I love God,' and yet hates his brother or sister, he is a liar. For the person who does not love his brother or sister whom he has seen cannot love God whom he has not seen. And we have this command from him: The one who loves God must also love his brother and sister. (Christian Standard Bible, 2017, 1 John 4:7–21)

CHAPTER 4

Jesus, the Lover

Love is the central, most important reality of who Jesus is in all His being and actions. Love is the principal motivation behind God's act of creation (Genesis 1–3 and John 1). Love in a relationship is what kept God from destroying all of humanity when we first, or any time since, rejected and opposed Him. Love is why God reaches out to us, inviting us back in. Love is the reason why God created us all, from the very beginning, with the capacity to *choose* or deny Him. Love is the very defining attribute of God (1 John 4) as it perfectly binds together all possible good attributes (Colossians 3) to their utmost degree. The heart behind the whole of God's Word (the Law, the Prophets, the poetic Writings, and the New Testament) is one of love—"*[Jesus] said to him, 'Love the Lord your God with all your heart, with all your soul, and with all your mind. This is the greatest and most important command. The second is like it: Love your neighbor as yourself*" (*Christian Standard Bible*, 2017, Matthew 22:37–39) (see also Deuteronomy 6, Joshua 22, Psalm 31, and 1 Corinthians 16).

So, how are we to view Jesus as a Lover? I believe the best example of all of this is found in the analogy of a marriage, as it stems from God having compared His people to a bride/wife throughout Old Testament prophetic words. Jesus is the perfect gentleman, the rider on a white horse coming to the damsel's (humanity) aid after she got (herself) into trouble. He seeks to redeem her, to restore her, and to present her to the King (God the Father) as a true lady, pure and exemplary. He persistently pursues her but never forces Himself on her. He proves Himself time and again but never makes the choice for her. He relentlessly makes His love and intentions known to her, knocking on the door evermore until she invites Him in. And one day, when the Father says it is time to have a wedding, and He will have considered her to be sufficiently courted, the choice will be considered final. He is also a jealous Lover—rightfully so, seeing as He is perfect and complete and only good. It would be nothing short of arrogant and rebellious for His lady to consider another (see Genesis 1 and 2, Exodus 20, Ezekiel 16, and Revelation 1 to 2). There is beauty in seeing Jesus as the courteous Hero in the pursuit of love. It answers many of the questions we may have about life and theology, or even theodicy (the questions of why God allows bad things) under the simple banner of "love, if not chosen by both parties, is not truly love."

We will look at finding a Biblical definition of "Love," then the instances in which Jesus addressed love, and lastly, conclude the precedent for love that He set for us.

What Is Love?

Ironically, it is not that you should not be hurt anymore (Haddaway, 1993). Love often deals with incredibly difficult matters in extremely harsh manners, which may often be necessary for any relationship to survive and withstand the trials that come with time. The Apostle Paul provided a very encompassing as well as poetic definition of love, which rests in the middle of his discourse to the Corinthian church on how to truly be a church of the true Christ: Jesus. See, we are very used to hearing 1 Corinthians 13 read at weddings as a celebration of love. However, that is a secondary applicability for these verses; their primary intent is on how Christ loves us and how we are to love one another within the church as a whole. Paul wrote this after Jesus' death, but it is a vital framework for a Christian to understand Jesus' lifestyle and attitude. Yes, we hear it so often we might be numb to the meaning, but if you truly follow the words, I think we all would have much better friendships and relationships.

Thereby, this foundational Biblical definition of love holds within it the following:

- Spoken words are only noise if not in love (see Genesis 1).
- Prophecy, or all knowledge, without love, is our undoing (see Genesis 3).
- Mountain-moving faith and a loveless heart make us nothing (see Numbers 20).
- Charity, chastity, or chastisement without love, gains nothing (see Romans 1–2).
- Patience (see 2 Peter 3).
- Kindness (see Matthew 8).
- Not envious (see Matthew 5:27–32).
- No boasting (see Deuteronomy 30).
- No arrogance (see Matthew 3).
- Not rude (see John 11).
- Not self-seeking (see John 17).
- Not irritable (see Matthew 14).
- Wrongs are not recorded or remembered (see Hebrews 8).
- Does not find joy in unrighteousness; instead only rejoices in truth (see Psalm 119).
- Bears through anything together (see Job).
- Believes anything that is given to each other (see Hosea).
- Hopes on everything to do with each other (see Daniel).
- Endures anything and everything as one, together (see Acts).
- It does not end or fade; it only grows and is perfected (see Revelation).

Three things can be considered to have the power to make external impacts. That is faith, hope, and love. Love, by far, outreaches and outweighs anything else in its eternal value. It is love that led God to *choose* to create where He had no obligation or request. It is love that led God to *choose* to fight to restore and keep a relationship with His creation. It is love that led God to make the ultimate call to bridge the chasm that we created between Him and us completely. It is love that enables God to endure His longsuffering patiently. It is love that, ultimately, will determine who will enter eternity with Him or apart from Him.

Jesus' Teachings on Love

Two key passages stand out for me on this: Mark 12:28–34, which I like to think of as a "Golden Rule" to understanding Jesus and His love, and John 13:34–35.

The words of Jesus in Mark chapter 12 were mind-blowing for people to hear at that time in history because many Jews were set on the Torah's "an eye for an eye." His true teaching is echoed in Matthew 5:38–42: Jesus asks us to turn a cheek from revenge and seek love. This stems from the commandment by Jesus to love one another. It was a foreign commandment for many at that time and still could be considered foreign today. This kind of selflessness is one of the purest forms of love. The fact that Jesus said this was the most important commandment shows how seriously we should be taking it in our relationships. Consider this the next time you deal with that annoying neighbor, co-worker, or family member; an act of love and kindness can go a long way.

In John chapter 13, Jesus called us to look different from the rest of the world, and this passage tells us we will look different if we love one another. Just as it is stated in Matthew 5:43–48, it is easy to hate, judge, or get angry with the person who cut you off on the road, the co-worker who makes snarky and judgmental comments, the homeless person asking for money on the corner daily, the neighbor who lets his dog poop on your yard and doesn't pick it up, and the spouse who doesn't do the dishes. I wonder what the world would look like if we decided to love these people instead of casting our hate and judgments onto them. Maybe we could open up a path to healing for them or a safe place for them. We understand life is more complicated than the above examples listed, and some people couldn't imagine loving the ones who have hurt them physically or emotionally. There are many people who live in daily abusive relationships, and what this verse is saying is not that you must remain in that relationship when it puts you in danger, but to continue praying for that individual. Enabling does not equal loving. If you are allowing the abuser to continue in his or her wicked and sinful ways, you are not loving them. You love this person by getting out of their sinful path and praying for their recovery. That is how you show love for yourself and others, following the heart of God to take care of His children as well as call all into His family.

The Love He Calls Us To

I believe the compilation of all the things written in Revelation is not as scary as many make it out to be. Yes, it may be difficult to map out a timeline—many church disputes have been started over this and the implicit meaning of various interpretations. I believe that this is given by Jesus to the church as a love letter, saying what He enjoys about His bride-to-be, what He misses, what He plans for her, and that He *will*, beyond any shadow of a doubt, be the one to come fetch her while still being there with her throughout any and all difficulty. It is the call of a Lover to ask His lady to wait just a little longer for His return, like a maiden at home receiving letters from her beloved out fighting a war that she only hears or catches glimpses of. In this, we can gather three things from Revelation, particularly chapters 2 and 3: what Jesus likes in His church, what He dislikes, and what He promises. This can be read like the summary of a couple's counseling sessions, where they remind each other why they love each other, talk about what they would like to improve about the relationship, and come into alignment on the same goals in unity.

What Jesus Likes in His Church

Jesus likes hard work, intolerance for evil, and patient endurance of this world. He wants us to examine the claims of those who call themselves "apostles," teaching things that may or may not contradict what He has said, thereby discovering any liars and lies within the church that could tear a divide between Him and us. He encourages us to patiently see any form of suffering through without quitting, like running a race with victory in our sights. Remain loyal to Him, refuse to deny Him, and do both at all costs. Fill our minds and lives with things founded on love, faith, and service, with a mindset of constant improvement. Ultimately, obey His word (living and daily, not legalistically) and don't deny it, for that would be to deny what He said and thus call Him a liar.

What Jesus Dislikes in His Church

Jesus dislikes when our love for Him decreases with time, when we do not continue to do the same things that we did at the start of our relationship with Him, and when we tolerate false teachings. He dislikes when we eat food offered to idols, thereby inadvertently agreeing with other religions and, in a way, accepting their false gods. He also dislikes any sexual immorality. As shown clearly in this chapter, the monogamous relationship between a man and a woman in marriage is intended by God as the best design (from the Designer) for us and is also meant to be a beautiful and holy illustration of His love for us; sexual sin defiles God's intention and illustration. When He sets a requirement for us, He knows it is one we can achieve, so when we fall short of that, it shows a lack of trust and faith on our part in Him. Jesus dislikes when believers are lukewarm: not actively denying Him, but not useful for anything good either. This is in reference to water that came to Laodicea from hot water springs via aqueducts—it would be lukewarm by the time it arrived in the city. This meant that it either had to be heated up or left to cool before it could be used. The only use they had for the lukewarm water was to make people nauseous and vomit, which is what Jesus compares this kind of unfruitful believer to. This links to the last and worst of all: indifference. They say that hatred is not the opposite to love, apathy is, and this is true by God's measurement through and through.

What Jesus Plans for His Church

Jesus plans for repentance, meaning to think of the things of God, not to fear suffering, and to be strengthened in anything we have left within or among us. He wants to give to us bountifully all that we need. He inspires us to do the works we did for Him at first and more, including returning to the simplicity of what was first believed, even if this comes with some loving correction and discipline. He promises us the right to eat from the Tree of Life in God's paradise, to live forevermore, and to be rulers in a new era under His reign. He promises a renewed state of righteousness, clothed in white clothes given, not washed or made ourselves, and that our names will be acknowledged before all of heaven, never to be blotted out in the Book of Life. He wants us to become pillars in God's temple, to have His Name and our eternal dwelling with Jesus inscribed on us, forever part of us, as we enjoy the right to be one with Christ as He sits on His throne evermore.

CHAPTER 5

Jesus, the Healer

In order to understand the full office of a Healer, we must have a comprehensive understanding of what the disease is that needs to be healed. We have all probably been in situations where a doctor seems to not know what is causing your ailment, but they start prescribing medication that would treat the symptoms and hope to figure out the cause along the way. While this is not, in principle, an incorrect method, this is a method based on more of a lack of knowledge than certainty. On the other hand, the expectation that would come upon an eternally omniscient (knows everything, always) being would be to have the exact answer to the cause and cure for the ailment.

Now, what is the true ailment? In the opening chapters of the Bible, it is clear that God's original plan was for humanity to live eternally and perfectly in harmony with Him. However, when we chose to disregard His recommendations and boundaries for a good life and wanted to make those decisions based on our own knowledge instead of trusting Him fully, we rebelled against Him and fell into the spiral of sin. God, being perfect and wise, knew that it would be devastating for Him and us if we were to still live forever, but in this state of making worse mistakes as days went on—sin compounds, as we see throughout human history. One bad decision by a stubborn, prideful, and generally unwise mere human leads to at least two more, with lies or dangerous events to add when left to our own devices. Look at stories with vampires—undead beings who are left with mistakes and remorse, who dig themselves deeper into their troubles the longer their "lives" dwindle on. Thus, death was "created" as a cure for sin, but it is the only true, or rather ultimate, ailment for all of humanity.

Every human ever born will die; that is a unifying fact. All other illnesses are symptoms of this core ailment. Sin is the true root behind all illness, death is the primary symptom, and our daily discomforts are secondary effects of this progressive worsening of human purity. For the believer, the inner and outer person (some refer to the spirit, mind, and body) are all connected and dependent on each other. Should one experience an issue, it will affect the other. The more we fall into sin, the worse the effects of that spiritual illness will sicken our minds and bodies. Maybe not all with the same results or over the same timelines, and definitely not according to a set mathematical relationship, but as there is a decline in the morality of a society or humanity as a whole, health soon follows. Thus, for Jesus to be the true Healer of all Healers means that He would restore, rectify, or cure the full scope of ailments from the deepest core outward. He had to come to undo the damage of sin to the spirit, out of which any other healing would flow.

There are three aspects that we can draw out of this perspective for further discussion into that worldview. What does spiritual healing look like with Jesus? What does physical healing look like with Jesus? And does Jesus still heal people today? These three would go hand-in-hand. Although we can split them up into separate focal points, once does draw from and lend to the others at the same time.

Spiritual Healing From Jesus

There are two subcomponents to spiritual health. First and foremost, spiritual health as a descriptor for our relationship with God—is it healthy, toxic, or non-existent? Secondly, the health of our inner person—the mind, soul, emotions, and so on. Jesus addresses both.

As we will discuss Jesus as Savior in more detail, He came with the primary focus of restoring our relationship with God to the fullness of what it should be. He showed us what it means to live with God in a healthy, sustainable lifestyle of holiness (a word that means "completely different, set apart, perfect," but based on the origin of it in the Greek language, also lends itself to an understanding of "taken out of an awful state and being brought toward perfection" (Bible hub, n.d.). This may include deliverance from demonic influences, possession, or surroundings, as we see Jesus do on a number of occasions—Mark even records this as one of Jesus' very first signs of being the Messiah. This addressed our primary spiritual health, removing all blockages on the metaphysical front between God and us by the forgiveness of sin and breaking the chains by which we were previously shackled to evil.

Jesus also addressed the secondary aspect of spiritual health with care and clarity. He promised to bring rest to the weary. He declared hope by saying that the yoke He calls us to bear is easy, and the burden is light. He took time to mourn the loss of His cousin, John the Baptist while remaining acutely aware of the will of God in the moment, according to His ministry and task at hand. He spoke against things like being anxious over what is not in your control, being overly concerned with future events, or being too fixated with other people's lives that you miss the true state of your own.

These two forms of internal healing often precede and, by all measures, outrank physical healing.

Physical Healing From Jesus

Jesus was known throughout the regions of that time because of His miracles, the majority of which consisted of healing people—some of the most controversial moments in His ministry happened because of Him healing someone from a sickness. What do you think your reaction would be to a man claiming to be the Son of God, restoring the sight of blind people, and telling lame people to stand up and walk? Or even raising people from the dead—a close friend, as well as servants and children of complete strangers, even those who might be considered "enemies" of his people?

From our perspective, Jesus seems to risk a lot in some of His healing. When we look at what He did from a human or legalistic perspective, like the Pharisees of His time, we might be tempted to find finicky details to "nail" Him on, like that He touched people with skin diseases. This could have been detrimental to His ministry and certainly added to the offenses that some took during His ministry. However, when we remind ourselves that it is completely unheard of for a man born blind to suddenly see, or a man born lame to suddenly walk, or a woman suffering from bleeding for more than a decade to instantly be of good health, or a little girl to sit upright after having just died, only then do we get the full picture of the physical healing. There is no formula, no checklist, no requirement rubric that we have to meet to "qualify" for God's miraculous healing. But when He does heal, He does it such that it serves a purpose—it makes Him known in truth and in love!

There is also no set pattern on how to receive physical healing from Jesus. Sometimes He prayed for people and other times, He just told them to do something. On occasions, He even just spoke it from a distance, and it happened. For the woman, He did not even initiate the healing (at least from the momentary perspective)—she touched His robe first! There is certainly no required amount of prayer minutes or recited Bible verses, and it does not rest in any person's arsenal. It is God, Jesus, and the Spirit who heal. The common denominator we do find throughout the whole Bible, and especially clear in Jesus' ministry, is that faith needs to be part of the encounter, either by expression of faith in the request to be healed or by God's plan to initiate and strengthen faith as a result of the healing, or both.

Does Jesus Heal Today?

Consider Matthew 15, around verse 30. Although Jesus performed many physical healings, he also healed many people spiritually. He also speaks of healing through rest to the tired (Matthew 11:28). How many of us are burned out and tired today? As Matthew records, it says, *"Then the news about him spread throughout Syria. So they brought to him all those who were afflicted, those suffering from various diseases and intense pains, the demon-possessed, the epileptics, and the paralytics. And he healed them"* (*Christian Standard Bible*, 2017, Matthew 4:24). He healed all manner of diseases and all manner of sickness. Addiction is a huge problem in our culture today, whether that is to alcohol, drugs, porn, sex, or money. Jesus is able to heal these as well—and He does! The Bible teaches how important our eternal well-being is and that when we go to Heaven, we will be made new with new bodies. Jesus valued our spiritual healing more than our physical well-being. If you are physically in the best shape, but your soul and spirit are a slave to sex or money, then you are distant from the relationship Jesus is calling you to—a relationship of eternal life. Many of us have hit our lowest point and broken self, and Jesus can heal that and restore your spirit and your faith. God wants you to thrive and use you for His purpose and King- dom. A wonderful consideration is the story of the paralytic man being lowered through the roof (Mark 2:1–12). It is a perfect example of Jesus healing us internally before healing us externally. The friends broke a roof open, lowered the paralytic man down, and Jesus first told him, "Your sins are forgiven," before telling him to get up and walk.

One last point of healing in all its possible forms that we can discuss is that of the community. See, when Jesus was going around the towns of Israel, ministering and healing, there was a large following of people who would also convey His teachings to these healed people. Afterward, when the Apostles took it further into the world, we see this principle as well—the healed people being incorporated into the believing com- munity in order to grow in their faith and be able to share it. Look at the following encounter:

Now Peter and John were going up to the temple for the time of prayer at three in the afternoon. A man who was lame from birth was being carried there. He was placed each day at the temple gate called Beautiful, so that he could beg from those entering the temple. When he saw Peter and John about to enter the temple, he asked for money.

Peter, along with John, looked straight at him and said, "Look at us."
So he turned to them, expecting to get something from them. But Peter
said, "I don't have silver or gold, but what I do have, I give you: In the
name of Jesus Christ of Nazareth, get up and walk!" Then, taking him
by the right hand he raised him up, and at once his feet and ankles
became strong. So he jumped up and started to walk, and he entered
the temple with them—walking, leaping, and praising God. All the
people saw him walking and praising God, and they recognized that he
was the one who used to sit and beg at the Beautiful Gate of the temple.
So they were filled with awe and astonishment at what had happened
to him. (*Christian Standard Bible*, 2017, Acts 3:1–10)

Now, continue to read through chapters 3, 4, and 5. Take into
account that this man was, literally, still hanging on to the shoulders
of Peter and John when that sermon was preached. Consider all the
people, the discussions, and the incredible burst of good things that
flowed out of this one healing.

The church is meant for each other. Healing is a gift given by the
Lord to edify, strengthen, and embolden the church in many different
ways. This includes freedom from demonic activities that still can latch
onto people just as in the days of the New Testament, physical and miraculous healing, emotional healing, and possibly even raising a person
who has just died from the dead. It's God's power, not ours; all we have
to do is be a vessel, be His hands and tongues in the world through
which He heals. Jesus promised that we would do what He did, and
even more and greater works, by the Spirit. A proper understanding of
Jesus as a Healer is to understand that He heals us perfectly, according
to His will, which is to unite us with God and one another. Armed with
that perspective, a willing heart, an open mind, and a strong faith in
the complete work of Jesus, we can believe, pray, and hope for healing
throughout the world and within the church today, and with a confidence that we will see Him do miraculous things in mysterious ways.

CHAPTER 6

Jesus, the Humble Servant

What is the difference between a slave, an employee, and a servant? A slave is forced to do something. An employee is remunerated according to the value of the work done. A servant chooses to do something without enforcement and with no expectation of receiving anything in turn—a good servant simply does what they do because it is the right thing to do at the right time. It is a choice to serve. When called into the military, in terms of crisis and war, when "all able-bodied men" are summoned, it is different from when one chooses to join the military out of your own initiative. Service is also meant to be a humble choice—a necessary choice, often, but still a choice. That is what Jesus' taking on the status of a servant was: a necessary choice to humble Himself from the status of eternal God to the stature of a skin-and-bone man.

The Choice

What was the choice He made, and why was it necessary?

Every time I think of Jesus' humility, I remember the climactic scene in *Indiana Jones and the Last Crusade*. He has to decide which cup is the "Holy Grail" to drink from and which one belongs to the King of Kings. He passes over all the shiny, bejeweled cups and picks the tarnished, faded clay cup saying, "That's the cup of a carpenter." The entire birth story of Jesus came from humility, with him being born in a manger because there were no guest rooms available. Jesus is a King and claimed to be a king, which means he could have had a much more luxurious lifestyle here on Earth, but humbled himself to travel with little to nothing, camp, and stay in people's homes (see Mark 10:45). The choice Jesus made was to discard all rights, privileges, and powers of being God in order to become fully man, live a life of struggle and hardship as a righteous human man, serve and minister to those around Him (especially in the last three and a half years, which were His public ministry), ultimately to die the most cursed and cruel death in the history of mankind, and be raised from the dead by the power of God and the Spirit.

That is no easy choice; in fact, even Jesus acknowledged it would be preferred if it could be avoided. On the night before His crucifixion, Jesus prayed.

Taking along Peter and the two sons of Zebedee, he began to be sorrowful and troubled. He said to them, "I am deeply grieved to the point of death. Remain here and stay awake with me." Going a little farther, he fell face down and prayed, "My Father, if it is possible, let this cup pass from me. Yet not as I will, but as you will." (Christian Standard Bible, 2017, Matthew 26:37-39)

So, why was this choice so necessary? Because for God to choose to serve someone, that choice is preceded by the mind-blowing, love-defining choice for *that person to exist in the first place*! Grasp this: The love of God is so much deeper than we could ever comprehend, but we can try. He loved so powerfully, planned and perfected each and every person throughout Human history, took ages to create the perfect universe, planet, and world for us to live in, and spent endless amounts of time with each of His people to get to know them. A love so deep it brings forth life! By choice! He *knew* we could, and would, turn away from Him, and He loved so dearly that He still made us. How does that make this choice necessary? Let any parent who chose to start having children with their partner tell you: Nothing could keep you from giving that person the absolute best that you ever could. God knows what is best for us, and nothing could keep Him from giving that to us—His love necessitated it! If He knew that He could restore the relationship, and He did not do it, it would mean He never truly loved us to begin with. The choice is a choice to love, which we addressed earlier, and true love endures anything and everything in faithfulness to the other.

So, why are all not saved? We will get to that in another chapter, but for now, rest in the understanding that a servant's service is offered freely; there is no contractual obligation, which also means the other party is as free to reject it as the servant is free to give it.

The Service

Now as you excel in everything—in faith, speech, knowledge, and in all diligence, and in your love for us—excel also in this act of grace. I am not saying this as a command. Rather, by means of the diligence of others, I am testing the genuineness of your love. For you know the grace of our Lord Jesus Christ: Though he was rich, for your sake he became poor, so that by his poverty you might become rich. (Christian Standard Bible, 2017, 2 Corinthians 8:7–9)

When Paul wrote this to the community of believers in the ancient city of Corinth, he did not have you in mind. He had no clue how far his work would reach, but he knew he had to do it faithfully and excellently. And his words ring true evermore to this day. Godly edification by the words of those led by the Spirit never fades. For Jesus, this was different. When He became a man, as He was growing up as a child, as He led His followers and ministered to people, and ultimately as He hung on the cross, He knew exactly how far His work would reach. He had you in mind. He denied all His glories and privileges for you to see that God understands you. He suffered through learning to crawl and walk and speak and read for you to hear what the true message of God is. He experienced pain, loss, betrayal, and death for you to know God feels what you feel. And then He became sin and satisfied the wrath of God, so you don't have to. That is love, chosen and seen through. That is servitude. A line I heard from a pastor preaching in church a long time ago has always stuck with me: "Strength is for service, not status." Your capabilities are not meant to elevate you above others but to enable you to love others better. The leader who thinks his position entitles him to be served by those who report to him will be corrupt and arrogant, mistreating, and will run what is given to him into the ground if unchecked—we have seen this in governments across the world time and again. A leader who understands that his position places on him the responsibility to serve those allocated to him, faithfully seeking their objective utmost best, will be successful and fulfilled.

Jesus also instructed us to love one another as He loved us. He showed us how to serve each other in the expression of that love. Consider John 13:1–15: Jesus washes the feet of his disciples. On that day, with the hot, dry climates, it was customary for homes to have water basins reserved for those who spent all day traveling in open-toed sandals, but this job was usually done by servants of the household. And it was a dirty, smelly process. As a blog post from Truth for Life (Begg, 2022) titled "Jesus Christ: Humble Servant" writes, "We see the glorious creator of the universe take the water He Himself had created and stood to wash His own creation."

When Jesus got baptized by John the Baptist, John himself objected to this, as he understood who Jesus was and felt unworthy to baptize him. However, Jesus being humble, allowed it. In fact, *"Jesus answered him, 'Allow it for now, because this is the way for us to fulfill all righteousness'"* (*Christian Standard Bible*, 2017, Matthew 3:15). This is often difficult to understand when we reverse-apply our latest understanding of baptism to this moment. A better perspective is to start with what happened at the cross. Jesus took all our sins on Himself and died the rightful punishment as the sacrifice of all sacrifices to settle the wrath of God. But that leaves us with no more debt, in an awkward limbo, where we certainly don't have the full kingdom of God yet (treasure, or priceless pearls, as He compared it in His parables). No, the full righteousness of Jesus, sinless and pure, was passed on to any who would receive it. Only the righteous enter the company of the Lord. When Jesus died, the veil that separated humans and the Most Holy part of the temple, where

God "dwelled," was torn from the *top* down. We have now been given a righteousness that enables us to commune closely with the Lord— but where did this righteousness come from? This righteousness came from a lifelong, daily, perfect, sinless, pure, loving, holy, and completely righteous lifestyle lived by Jesus alone. He did not just die for us; He lived *and* died for us. The baptism Jesus underwent was a sign to all of us of what He came to do. He did not come to be served but to serve. He did not come to be washed but to wash. His baptism was not to "wash off" the old life and take on the new life in unity with Christ, as Paul explains to the believers in his letters. The baptism of Jesus was to show the world that He, the Son of God, has come to meet us where we are at, to do what we could not, and to satisfy God fully on our behalf—hence the Spirit descending on Him and "*a voice from heaven said, 'This is my beloved Son, with whom I am well-pleased'*" (*Christian Standard Bible*, 2017, Matthew 3:17).

Jesus came into this world with humble beginnings and left with a humble death. Death by crucifixion was one of the worst and most humiliating ways to die. This is a reason why the cross is such an important fixture in this story. He could not just die; he had to suffer, both to feel and to visualize to us the long-suffering endurance God has gone through due to our sins. All of this was prophesied by David in Psalm 22, which Jesus references as He hung on the cross (they did not have book, chapter, or verse back then; they referred to passages by reciting the first few words), thereby owning that whole Psalm to Himself, declaring Himself to be the promised Servant of the Lord. This prophetic psalm speaks of the Lord's Servant and His life, suffering, and death unto God's planned victory. He received thirty-nine lashes because forty were known (or believed) to kill a man, and He had to be alive when they put Him on the cross. They normally didn't carry their own crosses up the hill, but Jesus was forced to do so, with additional beatings and mockery in the process. The crown of thorns was a sarcastic mockery and painful reminder of the Kingship He gave up to be the Servant He knew He had to be. The wine was a sour and bitter joke as He hung, dehydrated and bleeding, having to push Himself up by the nail through his feet just to breathe. This was no glorious death like the hero in a battle—this was a humble, slow, painful, thoughtful death. And He did it without a word of complaint or rebuttal. He did it with the utmost love.

With this perspective in mind, how well do you think you know Jesus? Does the heart and character of Jesus that you have attributed to Him fit these actions? How does what He did for you showcase who He really is? If the Word is meant to help us know the Lord closely and personally, how does this relate to passages you have recently read to introduce God to you more clearly? God gave His everything for you. He never had to, but He chose to serve and invites us to follow His example.

CHAPTER 7

Jesus, the Human

As we have progressed thus far, I think one thing has become evident: When we deal with a person, the lines between roles often cross or blur. This, perhaps, is further evidence that, as they remain consistent throughout, these aren't fictional constructs for a hypothetical or mythological person. If these were developed in isolation from a theoretical stance with an agenda, they might not have been so well connected without contradiction. The relationship between the different roles of Jesus we have looked at thus far seems to indicate something profound: He truly was a real *human*.

Jesus was fully human. The first point of this is that He was carried through a full pregnancy and born by a human mother. He was a baby completely dependent on his parents. He was raised as a child, among other children, in a few different but everyday communities. He probably went through awkward teenage years. And He worked a job as a carpenter. All of this made it difficult for people to believe in who Jesus said he was, especially when he went back to his hometown of Nazareth, as people knew him as a boy growing up there. Ironically, all these years later, we look to these human traits to support the view that He was (is) a real person (Ligonier Ministries, 2022) and why people *should* believe in Him for who He said He was (Ligonier Ministries, 2020). Where does your mind go when you read the following?

Then Jesus returned to Galilee in the power of the Spirit, and news about him spread throughout the entire vicinity. He was teaching in their synagogues, being praised by everyone.

He came to Nazareth, where he had been brought up. As usual, he entered the synagogue on the Sabbath day and stood up to read. The scroll of the prophet Isaiah was given to him, and unrolling the scroll, he found the place where it was written: "The Spirit of the Lord is on me, because he has anointed me to preach good news to the poor. He has sent me to proclaim release to the captives and recovery of sight to the blind, to set free the oppressed, to proclaim the year of the Lord's favor."

He then rolled up the scroll, gave it back to the attendant, and sat down. And the eyes of everyone in the synagogue were fixed on him. He began by saying to them, "Today as you listen, this Scripture has been fulfilled." They were all speaking well of him and were amazed by the gracious words that came from his mouth; yet they said, "Isn't this Joseph's son?" Then he said to them, "No doubt you will quote this proverb to me: 'Doctor, heal yourself.' What we've heard that took place in Capernaum, do here in your hometown also.'" He also said, "Truly I tell you, no prophet is accepted in his hometown. But I say to you, there were certainly many widows in Israel in Elijah's days, when the sky was shut up for three years and six months while a great famine came over all the land. Yet Elijah was not sent to any of them except a widow at Zarephath in Sidon. And in the prophet Elisha's time, there were many in Israel who had leprosy, and yet not one of them was cleansed except Naaman the Syrian."

When they heard this, everyone in the synagogue was enraged. They got up, drove him out of town, and brought him to the edge of the hill that their town was built on, intending to hurl him over the cliff. But he passed right through the crowd and went on his way. (*Christian Standard Bible*, 2017, Luke 4:14–30)

Moreover, an exercise we often forget to do, what do you think Jesus thought and felt at that moment? His people, His hometown, and the families He grew up with wanted to throw Him off a cliff. Jesus had real human emotions; he was hungry (Mark 11:12), he was tired (John 4:6), and he was sad (John 11:35).

So why is this important:

- We can relate to him.
- If we believe Jesus is the same yesterday, today, and tomorrow, then we have to believe the emotions he felt 2000 years ago are the emotions he still feels today. When we experience grief and exhaustion, he experiences it with us and can help comfort us in those times. If we believe Jesus is always with us, then we can conclude he is feeling our emotions with us. This goes back to Jesus as a friend. A good friend will laugh and cry with you, and that is the friendship Jesus wants with you.
- Jesus dealt with the same human temptations that we deal with but without sin. Only a human being can sympathize and understand these experiences because He, too, experienced them.

For a bit of deep theological thinking (speaking more to those readers who enjoy theology in its finer nuances throughout the context of church history), this becomes tricky when we try to define and figure out how this all works. From the very beginning, this dynamic between Jesus being God as well as Human has been a difficult topic for the church to define. It led to some powerful work by church leaders to come together and reach conclusions, such as the council of Chalcedon (circa 451 A.D). The church eventually settled on wording to describe this, based on the philosophy best known to them and the people at large at that time. They referred to the "nature" of Jesus—did He have one nature or two, or half of each? You can read up on the deeper philosophies, lengthy debates, and Scriptural analyses in this process, but the ultimate conclusion is that Jesus had *both* a divine and human nature. By extension, the question came about His "will" (Ligonier Ministries, 2019). The reasoning was that a person's will is uniquely connected to their nature. Jesus' divine nature is that of fully God, the eternal *logos*, which carries with it the fulness of the eternal, perfect, and divine will of God. However, Jesus has a human nature, which is that of being fully human and having been born, tempted, tired, hungered, and hurt. It is this will that we see reflected in His prayer in the garden of Gethsemane before His crucifixion. Jesus has two natures: He is completely God and completely Human. And He has two wills: He wills fully as God does, and He wills just like we do.

That is why He is the only complete and perfect bridge between humanity and God (in full, eternally, untainted, the Trinity complete). Jesus was human. He felt emotions just like we all do. He had a profession before ministry. He gets it.

Anything you are going through, He gets it! And He wants to be part of it. People often think they only have to pray and involve God when it comes to the "big stuff" in life. God doesn't just want to hear from you, like a postcard, when you are choosing a career, buying a new house, about to get married, or dealing with a sick loved one. He was on earth every day for about thirty-three years—He wants to hear about your day at work, your rest, your dreams, your meals, your joys, your traffic frustrations, your kids, your husband or wife, your passions and goals, and everything in between!

I sometimes say that God already gave us the answers to the big things. He set the boundaries of a safe and healthy life in the Bible, and within those boundaries, we have freedom in the best way because He guarantees His safekeeping and approval within that scope. Think of it like a sports field. The game is designed to be played within those lines and rules—they are there to protect you, the other players, and the integrity of the game. So, when you stick within the lines, and you know the rules, why is there a coach? The coach is there to help you with the small details, the momentary decisions, the current and next few steps of the game plan, and so on. God, in a way, has already covered the big stuff on our behalf. He wants to be part of the small stuff with us every day, all day long. Consider talking to Jesus with the consistency that you send text messages to a friend or spouse instead of a prayer life of only dedicated time slots like corporate meetings. Consider hearing His responses with the adamant but encouraging tone and frequency of a coach running next to you on the field.

CHAPTER 8

Jesus, the Savior

What is the definition of salvation? The Greek word for "Savior" stems from *soter*, from which the theological study referred to as "soteriology" is grown. This chapter would be a perfect opportunity to dig deep into those technical points and finicky details that theologians and apologetics love discussing for hours. But our wider focus here is getting to know Jesus. So, rather, we will be approaching the topic of Jesus being our Savior in the same way He did: He came to the uneducated and socially outcast, teaching in stories and parables. He made the gospel simple. There are three focal points in this simple gospel: Jesus, the eternally promised Savior, the theological understanding of atonement, and Jesus' complete character (all that we have discussed above) shown in His time on the cross, where the complete work of salvation was done.

First, let us discuss what our discussion of a Savior will, in a general scope, address. Most evangelists agree that, in order to tell people about Jesus as their Savior, the starting point is usually to establish the need for a Savior. The thing that separates Christianity, in all its forms, from all other religions is that all other religions tend to try and provide ways and means of earning your own best afterlife. Christians plainly acknowledge their sin and their inability to rectify that on their own. The Christian premise is that we are all aware of right and wrong, sin and righteousness (Romans. 1), and that any attempt to pursue good things will be tainted with sinful touches (such as selfishness, lust, envy, and hatred) that make even the good deeds with great intentions fall short of the best that God has in mind. The book of Romans is a brilliant exposition of the core foundation of the Christian faith, the full challenge of accepting the gospel, and is definitely a good place to start after reading at least one of the four gospels and the book of Acts (Theron, 2022-b). In it, Paul describes the dynamic of not being able to save ourselves by works of the law and offering our own sacrifices.

For no one will be justified in his sight by the works of the law, because the knowledge of sin comes through the law. But now, apart from the law, the righteousness of God has been revealed, attested by the Law and the Prophets.

The righteousness of God is through faith in Jesus Christ to all who believe, since there is no distinction. For all have sinned and fall short of the glory of God; they are justified freely by his grace through the redemption that is in Christ Jesus. God presented him as the mercy seat by his blood, through faith, to demonstrate his righteousness, because in his restraint God passed over the sins previously committed. God presented him to demonstrate his righteousness at the present time, so that he would be just and justify the one who has faith in Jesus.

Where, then, is boasting? It is excluded. By what kind of law? By one of works? No, on the contrary, by a law of faith. For we conclude that a person is justified by faith apart from the works of the law. (*Christian Standard Bible*, 2017, Romans 3:20–28)

Furthermore, the Christian stance is that our Lord Creator has a good, loving, and growth-filled life in mind for each of us (Jeremiah 29). So, regarding the question of the need for a Savior, there are usually two questions that come up first: "What do I need to be saved from?" and "What am I saved for?" To answer these questions, I believe the starting point would be to look at the person who claims to be doing the saving work and find His answer to these.

The mistake many people make is that we are being saved *from* God's anger and wrath. Even though this is clearly described as the destiny awaiting those who die in their sin according to the Bible, many think that this means Jesus and God are working against each other. Just before Jesus' public ministry, John the Baptist spoke to the Pharisees, those who religiously refused to enjoy or "live life" because they expanded even on the Jewish Law to rigidly uphold restrictions and rituals. He asked them why they were "fleeing" from the coming wrath (Matthew 3, Luke 3). Jesus echoes this in Matthew 23, where He exposes the hypocrisy of the Pharisees and scribes (these people were well-versed in Scripture) for not living what God truly intended with those sacred, written words that they recited so well. Many think that running to Jesus is meant to be just another form of fleeing from the imminent eternal hell that awaits us all as sinners. Rather, Jesus says to them and the whole audience:

How can you escape being condemned to hell? This is why I am sending you prophets, sages, and scribes. Some of them you will kill and crucify, and some of them you will flog in your synagogues and pursue from town to town. So all the righteous blood shed on the earth will be charged to you, from the blood of righteous Abel to the blood of Zechariah, son of Berechiah, whom you murdered between the sanctuary and the altar. Truly I tell you, all these things will come on this generation. Jerusalem, Jerusalem, who kills the prophets and stones those who are sent to her. How often I wanted to gather your children together, as a hen gathers her chicks under her wings, but you were not willing! See, your house is left to you desolate. For I tell you, you will not see me again until you say, "Blessed is he who comes in the name of the Lord"! (Christian Standard Bible, 2017, Matthew 23:33–39)

The Biblical answer is that God created us with freedom of choice, a will of our own that He does not (though He has the power to) overrule; His choice to make us from love meant that He honors our choices in love as well. If anyone chooses not to want to be with Him in this temporary life, He honors that choice in the eternal afterlife as well. The choice Jesus posed to us is not one of fleeing from hell, but for the first time since Adam and Eve, the choice was freely available to just run to God with open arms.

We also note that in Jesus' words in Matthew 23, those who are with Him and declaring His gospel are by no means experiencing lives of comfort. Another mistake many people make is to think that salvation comes with the assurance of everything in life going well, successful, untroubled, or with unending health and riches. A simple answer to this would be that if Christ brought us comfort, why would He send a Comforter after Him? (John 15). He also specifically promised difficulties, and, ultimately, He reassures us that it is not our perfection that He will reward but our perseverance (Revelation 2–3).

We are saved *for* a dual purpose: an unrestricted relationship with the Father, Son, and Spirit, and a divine calling to truthfully represent the God we now get to know personally to the world around us, unashamed and without fear of what the world might think or say. This is not just for the people many centuries ago in the Roman era, but even today, as can be seen in modern testimonies of believers in various countries (from the radical East to the liberal West). A wonderful example can be found in the story of one girl, Ashley, in an American college that Louie Giglio often talks about. The full story is available online (Ivan Bramlett, 2015). This is an easy task to grasp, but it is tough to follow through because it is regularly met with animosity and rejection since we are no longer privileged to the rights of this world because we are only tourist travelers (Hebrews 9–12) in this world now that our citizenship is that of the Kingdom of Christ.

Christ is the word we derived from the Greek *Christos*, meaning "savior." Christ is not Jesus' last name; they did not have family names like Smith or Oakley at that time. The person we know as Jesus Christ is a combination of His name (Jesus, which means *anointed* in Hebrew) and title (Christ, which means *savior*). Thus, let us look into those three aspects we mentioned earlier, pertaining to Jesus claiming and proving the office of THE CHRIST.

One passage that stood out to us, wherein Jesus speaks about His eternal being (John 8), touches on multiple facets of this topic. The discussion began with:

"Who are you?" they questioned. "Exactly what I've been telling you from the very beginning," Jesus told them. "I have many things to say and to judge about you, but the one who sent me is true, and what I have heard from him—these things I tell the world." They did not know he was speaking to them about the Father. So Jesus said to them, "When you lift up the Son of Man, then you will know that I am he, and that I do nothing on my own. But just as the Father taught me, I say these things. The one who sent me is with me. He has not left me alone, because I always do what pleases him." As he was saying these things, many believed in him. Then Jesus said to the Jews who had believed him, "If you continue in my word, you really are my disciples. You will know the truth, and the truth will set you free." (Christian Standard Bible, 2017, John 8:25–31)

Jesus is hereby identifying Himself as the One who sets all people free and simultaneously makes them aware of the fact that they are not currently truly free. He said that, even though they might be descendants of Abraham, they were not treating Him the way their father (ancestor) would have since they did not believe Him and even tried to kill Him. They went on trying to affirm their righteousness as children of Abraham, even children of God, based on their fleshly or moral claims, which Jesus gently opposed by their rejection of the plain truth He was presenting to them, which aligned with both God and Abraham. They resorted to trying to debunk anything he said and claiming that He was untrustworthy and a liar after He claimed to bring eternal life.

The Jews responded to him, "Aren't we right in saying that you're a Samaritan and have a demon?" "I do not have a demon," Jesus answered. "On the contrary, I honor my Father and you dishonor me. I do not seek my own glory; there is one who seeks it and judges. Truly I tell you, if anyone keeps my word, he will never see death." Then the Jews said, "Now we know you have a demon. Abraham died and so did the prophets. You say, 'If anyone keeps my word, he will never taste death.' Are you greater than our father Abraham who died? And the prophets died. Who do you claim to be?" "If I glorify myself," Jesus answered, "my glory is nothing. My Father—about whom you say, 'He is our God'—he is the one who glorifies me. You do not know him, but I know him. If I were to say I don't know him, I would be a liar like you. But I do know him, and I keep his word. Your father Abraham rejoiced to see my day; he saw it and was glad." The Jews replied, "You aren't fifty years old yet, and you've seen Abraham?" Jesus said to them, "Truly I tell you, before Abraham was, I am." (Christian Standard Bible, 2017, John 8:48–58)

The deeper significance of what Jesus said here is often missed by the first-time reader who doesn't know the context and philosophy of the audience these words were spoken to. The Jewish belief was that, in any standing, one's descendent is lower than oneself (Hebrews 7), which is what they are referring to with the "greater than Abraham," which Jesus specifically does not correct them on. Secondly, the "I am" claim Jesus makes is a title reserved by the Hebrew YHWH (reflected as *ego eimi* in Greek) as a title (basically a name) for God only, according to how God declared Himself (translated in different Bibles as "I AM that/who/what I AM") to Moses in Exodus 3. These two, combined, show Jesus unmistakably considered Himself to have come from an eternal existence with the Father, now incarnate as a man for our sake. Jesus making this claim was Him saying that He was the one who spoke to Moses and came before Abraham. By saying "I Am," Jesus is claiming to be God. This is the same God who saved the Israelites from the Egyptians and to the promised land. Jesus is claiming to be this same God.

Next, we will discuss the theological definition of atonement. We have briefly touched on this throughout the book and lightly broke ground on what we are saved from and for. We have seen that the Jewish community at large was expecting earthly salvation from the oppressive rulers, much like what David wrote in some of his Psalms while Saul was persecuting him. Jesus fulfilled all the promises ever made regarding God bringing salvation, but God's promise was based on the true human need and not our preferences or perception by self-diagnosis. In the Old Testament, the way to wash your sins clean was to offer a sacrifice. Innocent blood needed to be shed, most of the time in the form of an animal. The Jews had been practicing this from the start, as this was the only way to forgive your sins. This goes back to the Garden of Eden and Adam and Eve getting kicked out for not listening to God and committing the original sin. Because of this, we as humans could no longer live with God in paradise. This is where Jesus comes in. The Old Testament promises a savior for the Jewish people (actually, for all people). Jesus came as God in the flesh to offer the perfect innocent sacrifice to atone for all humankind. As Louie Giglio also explains in the video *Fruitcake and Ice Cream* (Ivan Bramlett, 2015), the beauty of the atoning work of Jesus is not just that He wipes away all the debt of our sin in God's "ledger" but that He transfers all the credit of His righteousness into our personal accounts—His perfect life now becomes our perfection. However, this is a gift, and gifts can be refused and can be left unopened. God is all-knowing because He does not experience time and thus sees all of human history in a single glance forever. He is also all-powerful because there is nothing that He cannot do—including restrain Himself from doing something. Many Christians develop a warped view of the atoning work of Jesus by thinking they still need to earn their way to the amazing, eternal life that God wants for all people—to say that this is a heresy is an understatement. However, too many Christians also sit too far on the opposite end of the spectrum, thinking that God pre-decided who will be saved and who will not and that He (Luther, 2017) guides their wills accordingly, such that "not a drop of blood from Jesus is wasted," as many of them will claim. This is also a heresy, I believe, since it denies God's love and expressed will to grant all people freedom and access to Him, as well as His eternal perspective by how it limits Him to linear timelines of cause-and-effect. Essentially, I believe the Bible is very clear on this: Jesus came to set all of humanity throughout history free, Jesus declared we need to only have faith in Him, and Jesus spoke of His true followers being those who live according to the indwelling Word of God.

The Bible also never speaks of anyone's name being "written *into*" the Book of Life, as many evangelists tend to preach on missionary outreaches, but only about "blotting out." This tells me that all people start off with the capacity, according to the desire of God, to live with Him eternally, and only choices to perpetually deny, reject, ignore, stifle, grieve, or blaspheme Him is what changes our path. Jesus came to set us straight on that path, to fix us onto the narrow road leading to the gate of life, which He said few actually follow. It is not an exact science, I think, to define a measurable moment of when any person is saved. The better approach, I think, could be to motivate all to get to know Jesus, to know what He did and said, to know who He is, and personally live closely with Him every day (Passion City Church, 2021). Let the Eternal figure out your eternity (Theron, 2022-a), and let we who are temporal focus on experiencing Him now, every day, every second, evermore. Atonement is Jesus bringing us back into right standing with God—he suffered so we would not have to, and I think we disgrace what He did if we are so bitterly sorrowful about our lives as "saved Christians." Enjoy the abundant life that He gave to you at such a costly price!

On the cross, the pinnacle of His salvific work to atone for all humanity, we see all these characteristics of Jesus show:

- The centurion, who witnessed crucifixions regularly for his job, declared, "Truly this was the Son of God!" as Jesus hung on the cross (Matthew 27:54).
- As Jesus walked to the hill, carrying the cross to his agonizing death, there were women crying and weeping for him. Jesus, as a friend, stopped to comfort them and show his concern for them and what the future holds (Luke 23: 26–31).
- Being a healer to a thief that hung on the cross next to him, saying, "Truly, I say to you, today you will be with me in paradise" (Luke 23:43). Jesus assured him that he was forgiven of his sins because he has faith in Jesus.
- As Jesus, the lover, was hanging on the cross, already beaten, bloodied, mocked, and humiliated by the Roman soldiers, He said, "Father, forgive them, for they know not what they do" (Luke 23:34).

- Jesus, as a humble servant, obeyed God and took up the cross, became a servant to sinners, and "humbled himself, and became obedient to death—even death on a cross" (Philippians 2:8).
- Jesus, in his human nature, bled on the cross, felt pain on the cross, and questioned God on the cross, saying, "My God, my God, why have you forsaken me?" (Matthew 27:45–51 and Psalm 22) as he breathed his last breath. Yet, He never wavered in His mission, character, or the deepest calling in His heart.

That is the love of God. The famous (possibly the most famous) Bible verse states that God so loved the world that he gave his only Son, that whoever believes in him should not perish but have eternal life (John 3:16)—THE SAVIOR!

Conclusion

Taking together these eight chapters with their various topics, references, and encouragements, where does your mind go? What has been the impression on your heart and the consideration at the front of your mind as you went along this journey with us?

At the outset, we said that the focus of this book would not be pure academic theology. Though that plays a role, it is rare that we go about our daily lives thinking constantly about the finer nuances of theology. What we experience daily is the presence of God. We are forever confronted with the reality of a Creator. We are regularly reminded of our small stature in the great cosmos while simultaneously being aware of the immense effects and massive magnitude of our actions, whether sinful or sanctified. Most people are constantly aware of a conscience, an implanted knowing of what is good, guiding our every step. We get to stretch, walk, sing, dance, read, work, love, write, laugh, drive, cry, and everything in between, all with different people, in different places, and expressing ourselves differently as days and weeks go on. Have you felt that there is, no matter how much things change, this unshakable constant that surrounds you and brings you certainty and steadiness? Like a compass or a strong tower, do you find yourself growing and changing and moving, and yet always aware of a singular constant, like a target you are aiming for? I hope and believe your answer to these questions will have been yes, after careful thought and honesty with yourself.

Our idea with this book is to introduce you, the reader, to Jesus. Yes, we may speak of historical facts from two thousand years ago, and we may be using words to describe Him that have developed and been refuted or refined over many years of church history, in philosophical circles, and in theological classrooms. Nonetheless, all the evidence in the world could not convince someone Jesus is real better than Jesus

Himself. Consider the passage below; how casual and joyful it would be to meet the risen Jesus in the same way His disciples met Him after He was raised!

Simon Peter, Thomas (called "Twin"), Nathanael from Cana of Galilee, Zebedee's sons, and two others of his disciples were together. "I'm going fishing," Simon Peter said to them. "We're coming with you," they told him. They went out and got into the boat, but that night they caught nothing. When daybreak came, Jesus stood on the shore, but the disciples did not know it was Jesus. "Friends," Jesus called to them, "you don't have any fish, do you?" "No," they answered. "Cast the net on the right side of the boat," he told them, "and you'll find some." So they did, and they were unable to haul it in because of the large number of fish. The disciple, the one Jesus loved, said to Peter, "It is the Lord!" When Simon Peter heard that it was the Lord, he tied his outer clothing around him (for he had taken it off) and plunged into the sea. Since they were not far from land (about a hundred yards away), the other disciples came in the boat, dragging the net full of fish. When they got out on land, they saw a charcoal fire there, with fish lying on it, and bread. "Bring some of the fish you've just caught," Jesus told them. So Simon Peter climbed up and hauled the net ashore, full of large fish—153 of them. Even though there were so many, the net was not torn. "Come and have breakfast," Jesus told them. None of the disciples dared ask him, "Who are you?" because they knew it was the Lord. Jesus came, took the bread, and gave it to them. He did the same with the fish. (Christian Standard Bible, 2017, John 21:2-13)

Throughout these various roles of Jesus, our discussion has been aimed at addressing how Jesus shows Himself to truly be the best of each of these. These are other people's stories, the testimonies of some people writing a book somewhere far away from where you are currently reading this. But Jesus is right there with you, always has been and always will be. The question is not whether you currently believe in Him or not. The question is not whether you want to believe in Him or not. The best question you can ask right now is not even one you have to ask yourself—it would be to ask Jesus to show Himself to you. Ask Jesus to show *you* that He is real. Ask Jesus to show *you* what it means to be a child of God since He bought our sonship as the firstborn at a dear price. Ask Jesus if you could get to know Him personally, as your Friend, as One who embodies Love, as your Healer, and as one who came to humbly serve all of humanity, including yourself. Ask Jesus if He would just walk the paths of life with you, like a true human, by your side, next to you in the car, at your desk, or having designated coffee dates. Everything in this book gives you an idea of who Jesus is and where to look for more clarity on who He is. But that means nothing if you don't get to experience Him for who He is. Not for who anyone has said He is or who some might want Him to be, but just plainly for who He is. He is faithful to keep His promises, to make Himself known, and to take care of those who call out to Him, to strengthen them with truth and love to be their best self. He has put an eternity of thought into making *you*. He is faithful to make each and every person their best self, a version of the self that only comes with a close relationship with Him.

As many as I love, I rebuke and discipline. So be zealous and repent. See! I stand at the door and knock. If anyone hears my voice and opens the door, I will come in to him and eat with him, and he with me. (*Christian Standard Bible*, 2017, Revelation 3:19–20)

Now, we pray that this book will have been a refresher, a starting point, for the reader. Now that you know, at least theoretically, who Jesus is, our request is to search out more Scriptures that give you glimpses into the heart, mind, and character of Jesus beyond just what He said and did. As you move along these verses, all throughout the Bible, do you see why so many find it beyond fulfilling to live a life with Him? Would you take up His loving invitation to know Him personally? To know Him in your own heart and life for who He has always been, as God incarnate, as Friend, as Love personified, the eternal Healer to all hurt, as humble Servant Who became human for your sake to be your personal Savior...

I am the true vine, and my Father is the gardener. Every branch in me that does not produce fruit he removes, and he prunes every branch that produces fruit so that it will produce more fruit. You are already clean because of the word I have spoken to you. Remain in me, and I in you. Just as a branch is unable to produce fruit by itself unless it remains on the vine, neither can you unless you remain in me. I am the vine; you are the branches. The one who remains in me and I in him produces much fruit, because you can do nothing without me. If anyone does not remain in me, he is thrown aside like a branch and he withers. They gather them, throw them into the fire, and they are burned. If you remain in me and my words remain in you, ask whatever you want and it will be done for you. My Father is glorified by this: that you produce much fruit and prove to be my disciples.

As the Father has loved me, I have also loved you. Remain in my love. If you keep my commands you will remain in my love, just as I have kept my Father's commands and remain in his love. I have told you these things so that my joy may be in you and your joy may be complete.

This is my command: Love one another as I have loved you. No one has greater love than this: to lay down his life for his friends. You are my friends if you do what I command you. I do not call you servants anymore, because a servant doesn't know what his master is doing. I have called you friends, because I have made known to you everything I have heard from my Father. You did not choose me, but I chose you. I appointed you to go and produce fruit and that your fruit should remain, so that whatever you ask the Father in my name, he will give you.

This is what I command you: Love one another. (Christian Standard Bible, 2017, John 15:1–17)

References

Baxter, R. (1860). *Gildas Salvianus: The reformed pastor; Shewing the nature of the pastoral work, especially in private instruction and catechising.* James Nisbet And Co. (Original work published 1656)

Begg, A. (2022, January 20). *Jesus Christ: Humble servant (1 of 7).* Truth for Life. https://blog.truthforlife.org/jesus-christ-humble-servant

BibleCodes. (n.d.). *Bible names code: Names from Adam to Jesus read as one prophecy.* BibleCodes. Retrieved April 3, 2023, from https://www.bible-codes.org/Names-bible-code-printable.htm

Bible hub. (n.d.). *Strong's Greek: 40. ἅγιος (hagios)—sacred, holy.* https://biblehub.com/greek/40.htm

BibleProject. (2014, October 1). *Messiah* [Video]. YouTube. https://www.youtube.com/watch?v=3dEh25pduQ8

BibleProject. (2020, October 29). *Who is Jesus?* [Video]. YouTube. https://www.youtube.com/watch?v=p7XRPGzL6kk

Bruce, F. F. (1983). *The hard sayings of Jesus.* Intervarsity Press.

Christian Standard Bible. (2017). B&H Publishing Group. https://read.csbible.com/ (Original work published 2017)

Daane, J. (1965). A time to re-examine method. *The Reformed Journal*, 17–20. ATLA Serials.

Edgar, B. (2017). *The God who plays: A playful approach to theology and spirituality.* Cascade Books.

Haddaway. (1993). *What is love.* [Song]. The Album. Coconut Records.

Ivan Bramlett. (2015, October 16). *4 fruitcake and ice cream* [Video]. YouTube. https://www.youtube.com/watch?v=VRX-CCp7e2O0

Jesus Film Project. (2021, November 17). *55 Old Testament prophecies about Jesus.* https://www.jesusfilm.org/blog/old-testament-prophecies/

Jones, T. P. (2015). *How we got the Bible.* Rose Publishing, Inc.

Jordan B Peterson. (2019, June 9). *On claiming belief in God: Discussion with Dennis Prager* [Video]. YouTube. https://www.youtube.com/watch?v=j0GL_4cAkhI

Kümmel, W.G. (1976). *The theology of the New Testament.* SCM Press.

Ligonier Ministries. (2019, September 14). *Does Jesus have one or two wills?* [Video]. YouTube. https://www.youtube.com/watch?v=bHJuFEHya2Q

Ligonier Ministries. (2020, March 9). *Since Jesus is God, who is a Spirit, how can Christ also be human?* [Video]. YouTube. https://www.youtube.com/watch?v=eboi7vbvUhs

Ligonier Ministries. (2022, May 7). *The person of Christ: Basic training with R.C. Sproul* [Video]. YouTube. https://www.youtube.com/watch?v=3zJ4lszc0Fk

Long, D. S. (2019). Thomas Aquinas' divine simplicity as biblical hermeneutic. *Modern Theology, 35*(3), 496–507. https://doi.org/10.1111/moth.12510

Luther, M. (2017). *Born slaves: The bondage of the will.* Christian Heritage. (Original work published 1525)

Passion City Church. (2021, May 17). *Don't give the enemy a seat at your table – Louie Giglio* [Video]. YouTube. https://www.youtube.com/watch?v=_mLgS63cObI

Pawson, D. (2017). *Unlocking the Bible: Charts, diagrams and images.* Anchor Recordings Ltd. (Original work published 2012)

Sproul, R. C. (2019). Who is Jesus? Ligonier Ministries. (Original work published 1983)

Strobel, L. (1998). *The case for Christ: A journalist's personal investigation of the evidence for Jesus*. Zondervan.

Theron, C. (2022-a). *The 3:16 chain: A brief journey along what the Word of God gives us within the 3:16 verses of each book in the Bible*. [Kindle Edition]. Retrieved from Amazon.com.

Theron, C. (2022-b). *The Romans Discourse: A brief unpacking of the logical flow of Paul's letter to the church in Rome*. [Kindle Edition]. Retrieved from Amazon.com.

Tim Mackie Archives. (2017, August 5). *Making of the Bible [Extended Version] Tim Mackie (The Bible Project)* [Video]. YouTube. https://www.youtube.com/watch?v=eaqKzYJ151Y

Windle, B. (2022, November 18). *Top ten historical references to Jesus outside of the Bible*. Bible Archaeology Report. https://biblearchaeologyreport.com/2022/11/18/top-ten-historical-references-to-jesus-outside-of-the-bible/

Milton Keynes UK
Ingram Content Group UK Ltd.
UKHW020627140823
426838UK00016B/833